CHAIR YOGA
FOR SENIORS

SONYA RAIMOND

Copyright © 2024

All rights reserved worldwide

No part of this book may be reproduced or transmitted in any form or by any means, electronic or mechanical, including photocopying, recording or by any information storage and retrieval system, without written permission from the publisher, except for the inclusion of brief quotations in a review.

Warning-Disclaimer

The purpose of this book is to educate and entertain. The author or publisher does not guarantee that anyone following the techniques, suggestions, tips, ideas, or strategies will become successful. The author and publisher shall have neither liability or responsibility to anyone with respect to any loss or
damage cause, or alleged to be cause, directly or indirectly by the information contained in this book

Please Give Us Your **FEEDBACK!**

★ ★ ★ ★ ★

SCAN ME

A FREE BONUS IS WAITING YOU!

Join NOW our newsletter!

SCAN ME

Table of Contents

INTRODUCTION: Reclaim your youth and independence.................... 1
CHAPTER 1: How to improve your mobility................................ 3
CHAPTER 2: Chair yoga for weight loss................................... 6
WARM-UP SEQUENCES:... 8
Neck Extension and Flexion 9
Seated Neck Turn.. 10
Seated Neck Tilt.. 11
Seated Shoulder Roll.. 12
Cross-Body Arm Stretch.. 13
Chair Eagle Arms.. 14
Side-Seated Chair Twist... 15
Seated Ankle Rotations.. 16
Seated Chair Twist.. 17
Sit-Ankle Stretch... 18
Wrist Flexor Stretch.. 19
Seated Toe Tapping.. 20
Seated Wrist Rotations.. 21
Chair Cat-Cow Stretch... 22
CARDIO BOOSTERS FOR WEIGHT LOSS:..25
Seated Skaters.. 26
Seated Leg Swings... 27
Twist and Shout... 28
Seated Side Steps... 29
Seated Jumping Jacks 30... 30
Chair Sprints... 31

Arm Circles.. 32
Seated Side Leg Lifts... 33
Seated Toe Touches.. 34
Chair Mountain Climbers... 35
MUSCLE TONING FOCUS:..**36**
Seated Overhead Press... 37
Chair Push-Ups.. 38
Seated Tummy Twists.. 39
Chair Squats.. 40
Seated Side Leg Lifts... 41
Seated Leg Curls... 42
Seated Leg Presses.. 43
Chair Dips.. 44
Seated Cross Crunche.. 45
CORE ACTIVATION AND BALANCE:......................................**48**
Seated Side Twists.. 49
Standing Leg Curl.. 50
Seated Leg Extensions.. 51
Chair Balance Lift.. 52
Seated Bicycle Crunches.. 53
Chair Boat Pose... 54
Seated Marches.. 55
Chair Taps... 56
UPPER BODY STRENGTH AND FLEXIBILITY:.......................**57**
Seated Star Twist.. 58
Seated Overhead Stretch.. 59
Seated Bicep Stretch.. 60
Chair Tricep Stretch.. 61

Seated Chest Expansion.. 62
LOWER BODY STRENGTH & FLEXIBILITY:.. 65
Seated Leg Lifts... 66
Hamstring Stretch.. 67
Chair Pigeon Pose... 68
Chair Ankle Flex.. 69
Seated Calf Raises.. 70
28-DAYS PLAN: Full Body Mobility... 71
28-DAYS PLAN: Weight Loss.. 73

Reclaim your youth and independence

Welcome! Together we will go on this delightful adventure through chair yoga to regain vitality, improve mobility, and lose weight. In this introductory chapter, we will explore the transformative power of chair yoga and how it can be an effective means of slowing the aging process and reclaiming that feeling of youth that we may have thought was lost.

As we age, it is common to feel less energetic and dynamic. Mobility decreases, muscles weaken and flexibility decreases. However, yoga offers an accessible and adaptable solution to these challenges. Through a series of postures and movements designed specifically to be performed in the chair, it is possible to improve joint mobility, strengthen muscles, and increase flexibility while simultaneously losing weight, regardless of age or physical ability.

As you will see below, yoga is a powerful ally in the fight against excess weight. Through a combination of dynamic and static movements, you can boost metabolism, burn calories and tone muscles, thus contributing to sustainable weight loss over time.

But the goal is not just to achieve a number on the scale; it is also about reconnecting with your body, developing a positive relationship with food, and learning how to eat healthily and mindfully.

Well yes, because yoga is not just limited to the physical body; it also works on the mind and spirit. Breathing practices can help reduce stress, improve concentration and promote an overall sense of well-being. This holistic approach is key to regaining vitality and counteracting aging

Throughout this book, we will explore in detail the various aspects briefly introduced just now and how they can be integrated into your daily routine to improve your overall health and well-being. Whether you are looking to improve your mobility, lose weight, or simply feel younger and more vital, chair yoga can be your ideal companion along this transformative path. Get ready to release your inner youthfulness and embrace a life full of vitality,

How to improve your mobility

Mobility is critical to maintaining an active and independent lifestyle. When mobility decreases, daily activities can become more difficult and quality of life can drop dramatically. In this chapter, we will explore how chair yoga can be a powerful tool to improve your mobility, increase flexibility, and restore natural joint movement.

- **Evidence through scientific studies and research:** Chair yoga is supported by scientific evidence for its effectiveness in improving mobility. One of the most important researches was conducted at Harvard Medical University (Jones et al., 2018) and showed the benefits of chair yoga in improving the mobility of people with knee arthritis. Another study published in the Journal of Aging and Physical Activity (Smith et al., 2019) showed that an eight-week chair yoga program led to significant improvement in joint flexibility and mobility in the elderly.

- **Understanding mobility:** First, it is important to understand what is meant by mobility and why it is important. Mobility refers to the ability to move freely and painlessly through a full range of motion in joints. Good mobility is essential for performing daily activities, such as bending, rising from a chair, walking, and climbing stairs, safely and efficiently.

- **Benefits of chair yoga on mobility:** Chair yoga is a low-impact form of exercise that can be adapted for people of all ages and skill levels. Yoga postures and movements aim to improve flexibility, strength and balance, all of which are crucial. We will explore how these yoga practices reduce the risk of stiffness and pain.

- **Specific exercises:** In the following chapters, we will present a series of exercises designed specifically to improve mobility that aim to work on different parts of the body, including the spine, shoulders, hips and knees. Through a combination of gentle movements and stretching, you will learn how to increase your flexibility and reduce muscle tension, thereby improving your ability to move freely and painlessly.

Not only can this approach to exercise help you achieve greater range of motion, it can also improve your overall quality of life, making you able to perform daily activities with greater ease and comfort, reducing the risk of falls and injuries.

When you start practicing exercises, it is important to be patient and consistent in your efforts. The benefits will not come overnight, but with regular practice and attention to proper technique, you will begin to notice improvements within a few weeks.

In addition, these exercises can be easily adapted to your needs and skill level. If you have physical limitations or are just starting out, you can start with easier positions and gradually increase the challenge as you gain confidence and strength. It is important to listen to your body and respect its limits, avoiding pushing yourself too far and causing injury.

Finally, remember to focus on your breathing and bring awareness to your body through the sensations you experience during the exercises. This mindfulness approach can help reduce stress and anxiety, further improving your overall well-being.

Get ready and set out on this journey with dedication you will see the benefits reflected not only in your body, but also in your mind and spirit!

Chair yoga for weight loss

In the previous chapter, we explored how chair yoga can improve your mobility and increase joint flexibility. Now, we will focus on how this powerful tool can be used for weight loss safely and effectively.

- **Evidence through scientific studies and research:** Chair yoga is supported by scientific evidence for its effectiveness in weight loss. A study conducted at the University of Applied Sciences in Berlin (Müller et al., 2021) examined the effects of a chair yoga program on body composition and metabolism in overweight individuals. Results showed a significant reduction in body fat and improvement in metabolism after eight weeks of regular chair yoga practice.

- **Understanding weight loss:** First, it is important to understand the fundamentals of weight loss. Weight loss occurs when you create a caloric deficit, that is, you consume fewer calories than you take in. However, it is not only about reducing calories but also about creating a healthy and sustainable lifestyle that promotes long-term weight loss.

- **Role of yoga in weight loss:** Chair yoga can be a valuable component of a weight loss program. While you may not burn the same amounts of calories as you would with a high-intensity workout, chair yoga can still help you lose weight in several ways. First, the exercises can help tone your muscles and increase your metabolism, which can lead to increased calorie burning even at rest. In addition, it can help reduce stress and anxiety, which can be contributing factors to weight gain.

- **Specific yoga exercises for weight loss:** In the following chapters, we will explore several exercises specifically designed to promote weight loss. These will include dynamic movements that involve multiple muscle groups and can increase the heart rate to burn calories. We will also incorporate balancing and stabilizing positions that can help you develop muscle strength and endurance, thus improving your ability to perform more challenging exercises over time.

Now that you clearly understand how chair yoga can be an effective option for weight loss, start practicing the proposed exercises with commitment and determination and you will see the results reflected not only on the scale, but also in your health and mental well-being.

WARM-UP SEQUENCES

YOGA FOR SENIORS

Neck Extension and Flexion

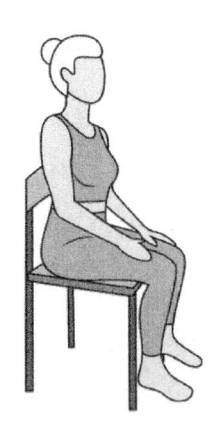

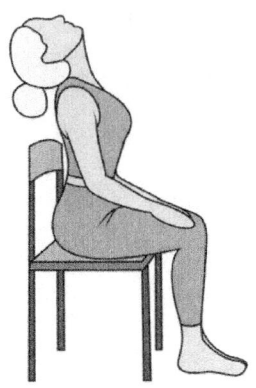

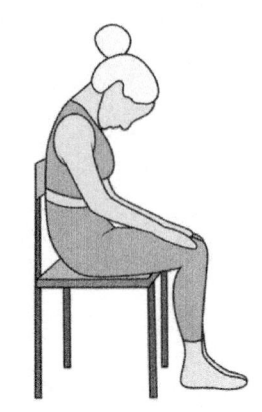

1. How to do it

- Begin by sitting with a straight back and hands resting on your lap
- Gently tilt your head back to gaze at the ceiling for extension
- Next, bring your chin towards your chest for flexion

2. Breathing

- Breathe in while tilting your head back
- Breathe out as you come back to the center
- Exhale as you bring your chin towards your chest

3. Tips

- Avoid sudden or jerky movements while exercising
- If you have a history of neck issues, exercise caution and seek advice from a healthcare professional

EASY

Seated Neck Turn

YOGA FOR SENIORS

1. *How to do it*

- Sit in a chair with feet flat, spine straight
- Tilt head right, ear to shoulder for a neck stretch
- Return head to center and repeat on left side

2. *Breathing*

- Breathe in while keeping your head centered
- Exhale slowly as you tilt your head to one side
- Inhale as you bring your head back to the center

3. *Tips*

- To prevent lifting the opposite shoulder, remember to keep your shoulders relaxed and down while tilting your head
- If you feel any sharp pain, discontinue the stretch right away

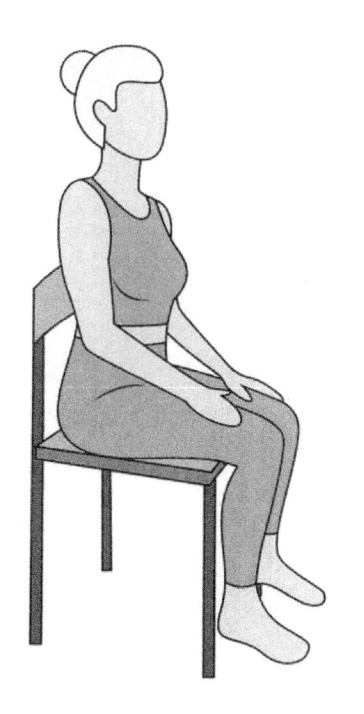

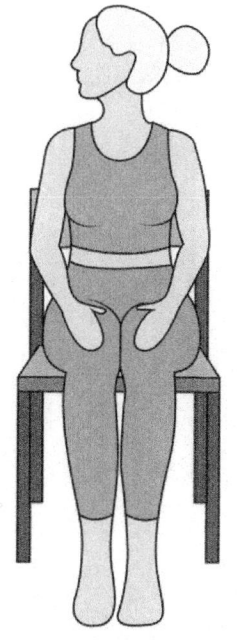

EASY

YOGA FOR SENIORS

Seated Neck Tilt

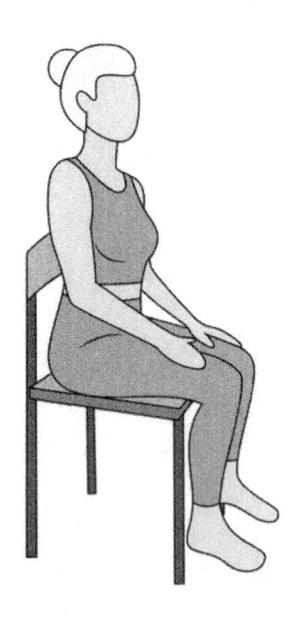

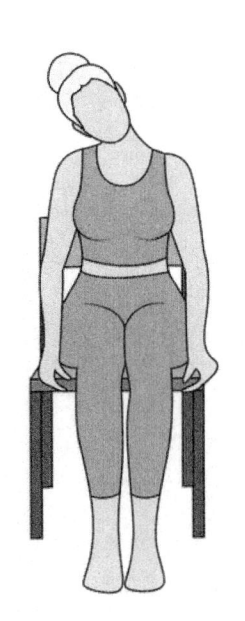

1. *How to do it*

- Sit comfortably with feet flat, spine erect
- Slowly tilt head to right, ear to shoulder, feeling a stretch
- Return to center and repeat on left side

2. *Breathing*

- Breathe in while maintaining your head in the center position
- Exhale slowly as you tilt your head to one side
- Inhale as you come back to the center position

3. *Tips*

- Keep shoulders relaxed and down when tilting head to avoid lifting the opposite shoulder
- If you experience sharp pain, stop the stretch immediately.

EASY

Seated Shoulder Roll

1. How to do it

- Sit upright with feet flat on the floor

- Raise your shoulders towards your ears, then roll them back, squeezing your shoulder blades together

- Lower your shoulders and roll them forward. Repeat in opposite direction

2. Breathing

- Inhale while lifting shoulders up

- Exhale as you finish the backward roll, lowering shoulders

- Inhale to begin rolling forward

- Exhale to complete the forward roll

3. Tips

- Maintain a straight spine and relaxed neck to prevent jerky movements

- Ensure that the movement is smooth and controlled

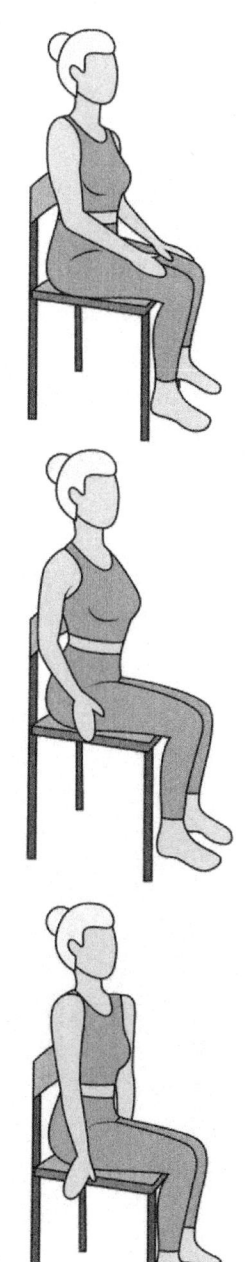

EASY

YOGA FOR SENIORS

Cross-Body Arm Stretch

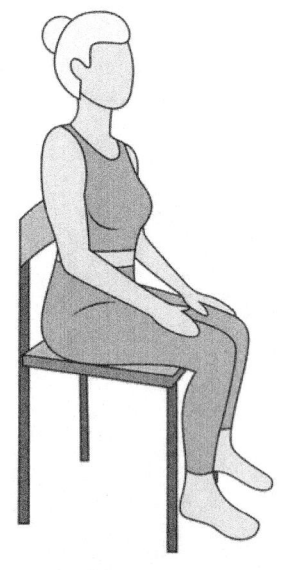

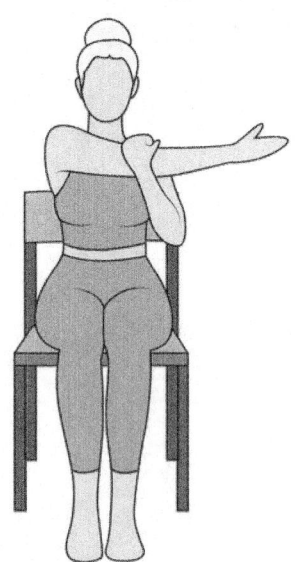

1. *How to do it*

- Sit down and stretch your right arm across your body
- Holding the position for a few breaths to experience a gentle stretch in the back of the shoulder
- Repeat the same on the left side

2. *Breathing*

- Before starting the stretch, take a deep breath
- Exhale as you pull your arm across your body
- Keep your breathing natural while holding the position
- Inhale when releasing the arm and switching sides

3. *Tips*

- Ensure a straight spine and avoid leaning
- Stretch gently without discomfort or excessive force

EASY

Chair Eagle Arms

YOGA FOR SENIORS

1. How to do it

- Sit comfortably with a straight spine
- Cross arms, right over left, then left over right
- Lift elbows slightly and push hands away for a stretch
- Repeat on both sides to balance the stretch.

2. Breathing

- Extend your arms as you inhale
- Wrap your arms and settle into the pose as you exhale
- Take a deep breath while holding the position
- Exhale as you release and get ready to switch sides

3. Tips

- Provide alternative poses for those with limitations, such as crossing arms instead of a full wrap
- Avoid sharp pain and stretch comfortably.

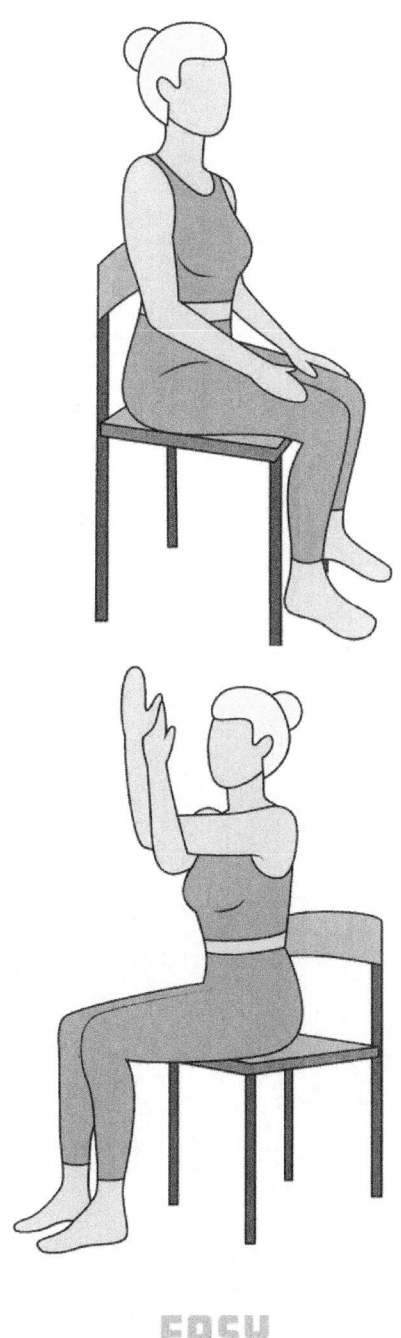

EASY

YOGA FOR SENIORS | 14

Side-Seated Chair Twist

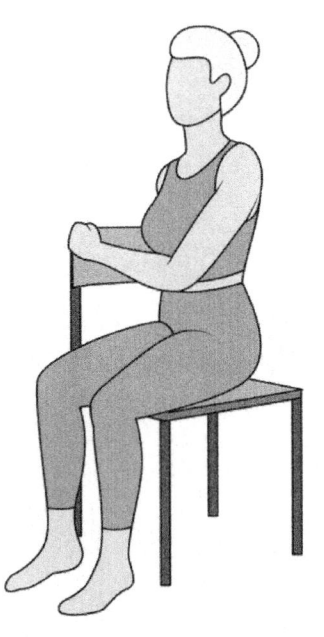

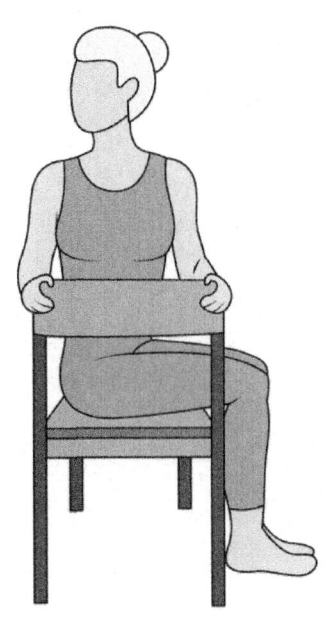

1. How to do it

- Reposition sideways on chair,
- Inhale deeply to lengthen spine
- Exhale and twist gently
- Hold for a few breaths, then switch sides.

2. Breathing

- Inhale to elongate the spine before twisting
- Exhale gently as you twist
- Maintain deep and natural breathing during the twist
- Inhale while releasing and getting ready to switch sides

3. Tips

- Maintain a straight spine and refrain from leaning backward or forward
- When twisting, avoid excessive force or using the arms; the movement should be gentle

EASY

Seated Ankle Rotations

1. How to do it

- Ensure you sit upright in your chair with your feet flat on the floor

- Extend your right leg forward, keeping the heel on the floor

- Rotate your right ankle slowly in a clockwise direction for a few rounds, then switch to counterclockwise

2. Breathing

- Begin the rotation by inhaling

- Complete one round of rotation by exhaling.

3. Tips

- Make sure the movement is deliberate and steady

- Opt for a gentle rotation rather than a forceful one to prevent injury.

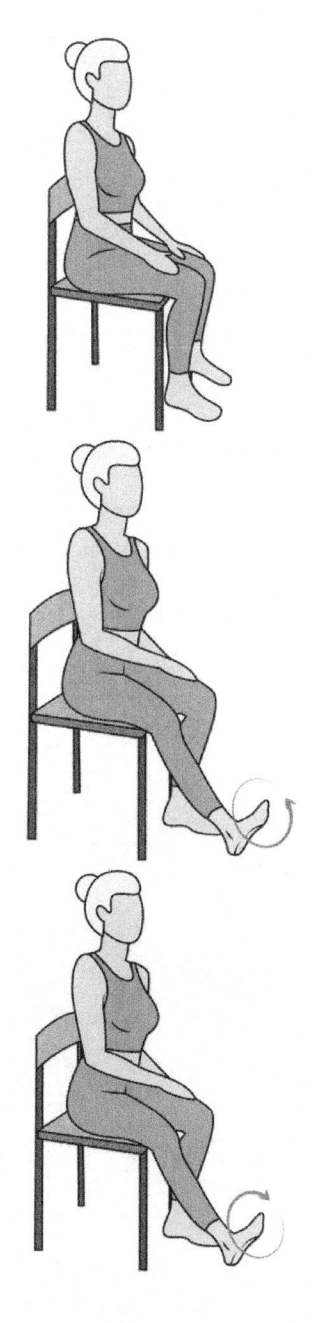

EASY

YOGA FOR SENIORS

Seated Chair Twist

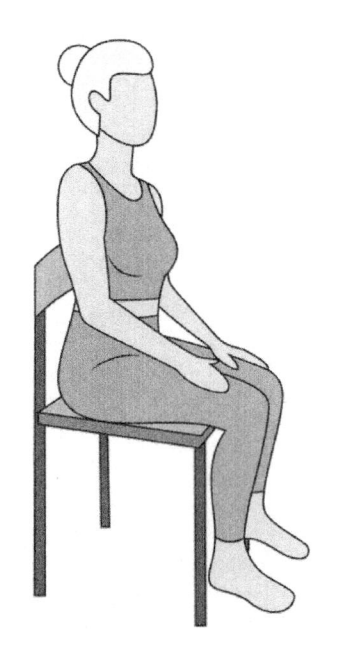

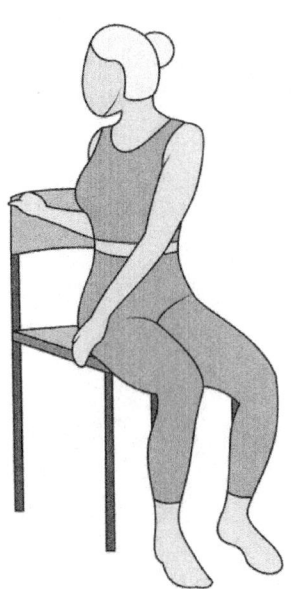

EASY

1 *How to do it*

- Sit upright with feet flat and hip-width apart

- Place left hand on right armrest, right hand on chair back

- Inhale, lengthen spine, exhale while twisting right, looking over right shoulder

- Hold, then return to center and repeat on the left side

2 *Breathing*

- Take a deep breath to get ready for the twist

- Exhale while twisting to one side

- Maintain natural breathing throughout the twist

- Inhale as you come back to the center

3 *Tips*

- Remember to twist from the base of your spine to avoid neck strain

- Keep both hips on the chair to prevent excessive twisting

Sit-Ankle Stretch

1. How to do it

- Sit down and stretch your right leg straight out in front of you

- Flex your ankle by pointing your toes up towards the ceiling

- Next, point your toes away from you to stretch the top of your foot

2. Breathing

- Breathe in as you flex your ankle

- Breathe out as you point your toes away

3. Tips

- Keep the leg stationary and only move the ankle

- Ensure smooth transitions and avoid sudden, jerky movements

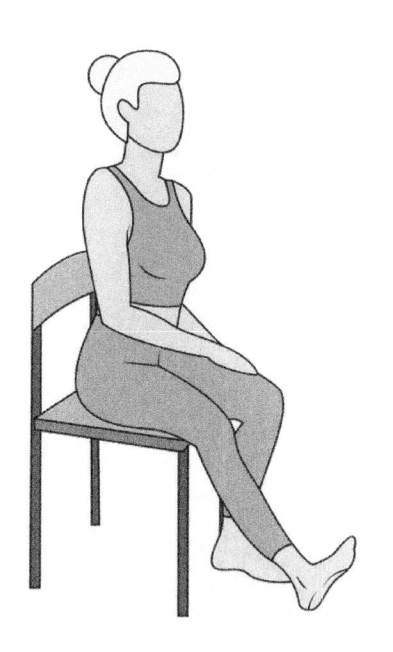

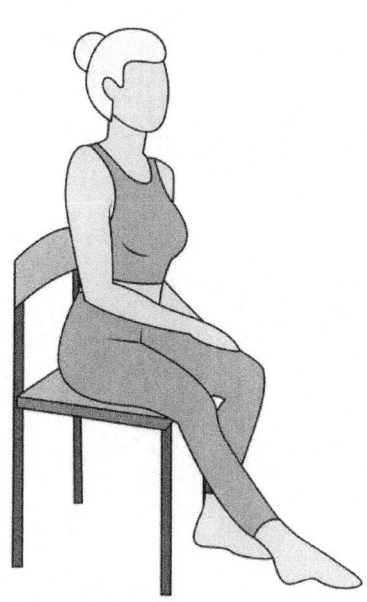

EASY

YOGA FOR SENIORS

Wrist Flexor Stretch

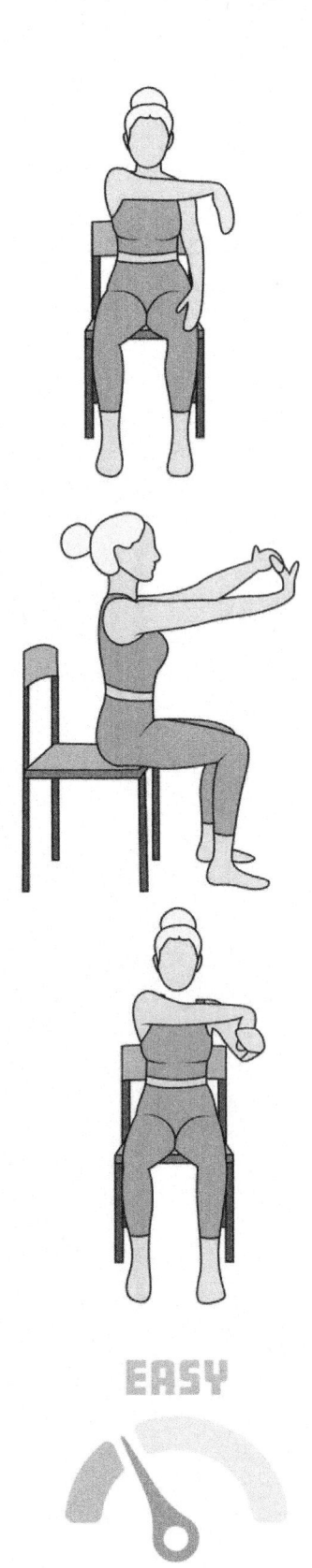

1. How to do it

- Stretch your right arm forward at shoulder level, palm up
- Gently pull fingers towards the forearm for 30 seconds
- Repeat with palm down
- Switch arms and repeat.

2. Breathing

- Take a deep breath while extending your arm
- Exhale slowly while gently stretching
- Inhale once more as you release

3. Tips

- Stretch the wrist and forearm gently without causing pain by keeping the arm extended straight and bending only the wrist
- Be cautious not to overstretch

EASY

Seated Toe Tapping

1. How to do it

- Find a comfortable seating position with your feet flat on the floor

- While keeping your heels down, raise the toes of both feet and then gently tap them back down

- Repeat this tapping movement in a rhythmic manner

2. Breathing

- Inhale while lifting your toes

- Exhale while lowering them back down

3. Tips

- To avoid strain, concentrate on moving from the ankles instead of the whole leg

- Ensure that the movement is gentle to protect your foot muscles from overexertion.

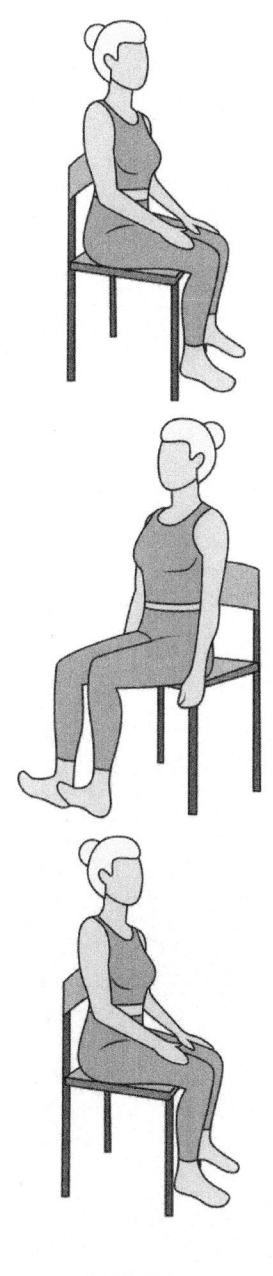

EASY

Seated Wrist Rotations

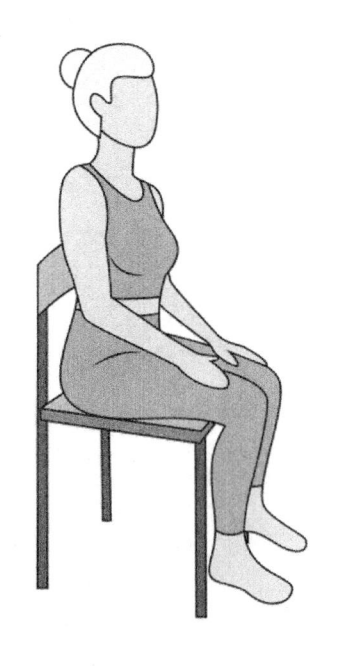

1. How to do it

- Sit upright with feet flat, hip-width apart
- Extend arms at shoulder height, palms down
- Make fists and rotate wrists in circular motions for 30 seconds each direction

2. Breathing

- Begin by taking a deep breath
- Exhale consistently while rotating
- Inhale once more when altering the rotation direction
- Remember not to hold your breath

3. Tips

- Focus on moving only your wrists, without engaging your entire arm
- Keep your shoulders relaxed and still to avoid them from lifting.

EASY

Chair Cat-Cow Stretch

1 How to do it

- Sit at the front of the chair with feet flat, hands on knees.
- Inhale to arch back into cow position
- Exhale to round spine into cat position.

2 Breathing

- Take a deep breath while doing the cow stretch (arching)
- Exhale as you perform the cat stretch (rounding).

3 Tips

- Make sure that movements are coordinated smoothly with the breath
- Avoid putting strain on the neck; opt for gentle and fluid movements

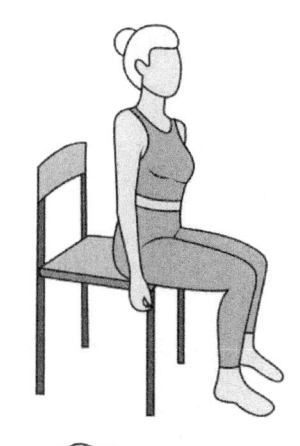

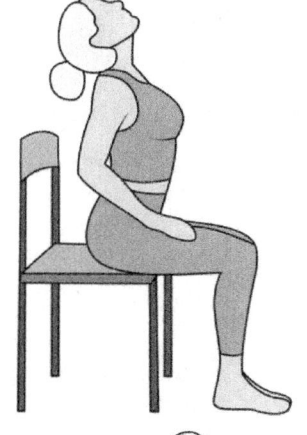

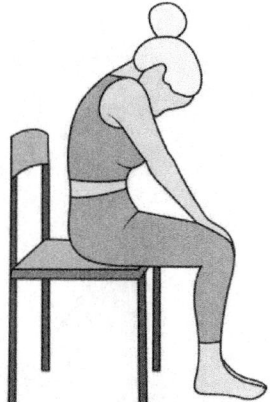

EASY

Please
Give Us Your
FEEDBACK!

★★★★★

SCAN ME

A FREE BONUS IS WAITING YOU!

Join NOW our newsletter!

SCAN ME

CARDIO BOOSTERS FOR WEIGHT LOSS

Seated Skaters

1. How to do it

- Sit at the edge of your chair with your feet flat and slightly apart

- Extend your left leg out to the side with your toes pointed

- Lean forward slightly and reach your left arm inside your right foot while raising your right arm behind your body, twisting through your torso. Repeat on the other side for one full repetition

2. Breathing

- Straighten up, deep inhale

- Exhale while twisting and extending leg, switch sides, repeat

3. Tips

- Keep back straight while twisting, engage core for stability

- Control leg extension

- Twist from midsection with elongated spine

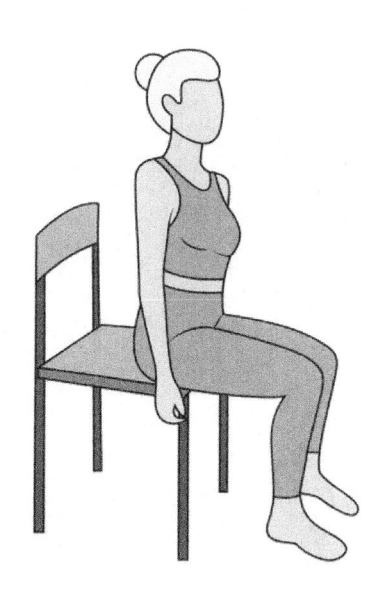

MEDIUM

Seated Leg Swings

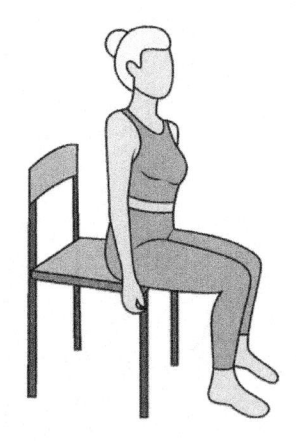

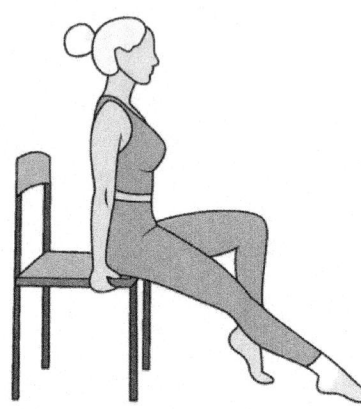

1. *How to do it*

- Sit upright on a stable chair with feet flat on the floor
- Use hands on chair or lap for stability
- Lift right leg to hip level, swing it back without bending knee
- Repeat swinging motion, then switch to left leg

2. *Breathing*

- Inhale while swinging the leg forward
- Exhale while swinging it backward

3. *Tips*

- Maintain a straight back and activate your core muscles to stay balanced
- Focus on executing smooth and controlled movements, steering clear of relying on momentum

EASY

Twist and Shout

1. How to do it

- Sit upright in a chair, feet flat on the floor, arms extended
- Twist torso right, head turning to look over right shoulder
- Right arm reaching back of chair, left arm extending front
- Return to center and repeat on left side in a smooth, rhythmic motion.

2. Breathing

- Inhale deeply in the center position
- Exhale as you twist to each side

3. Tips

- To prevent lower back strain, ensure your hips and seat remain in the chair
- The term "shout" is metaphorical, representing the exuberant expression of the movement

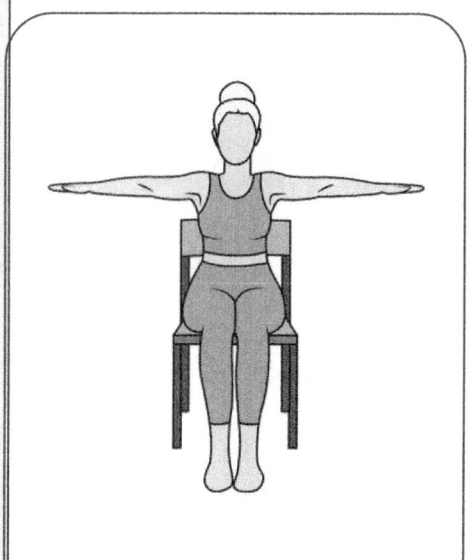

EASY

Seated Side Steps

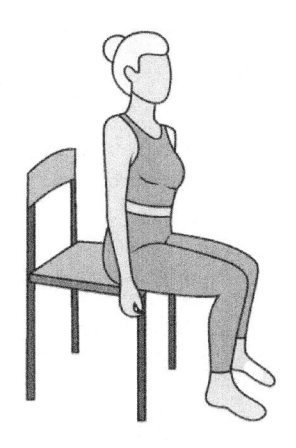

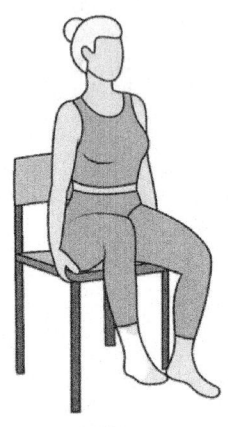

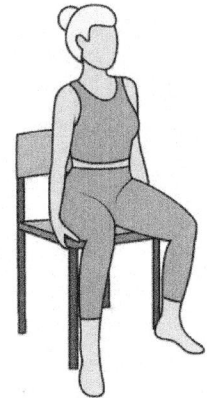

1. How to do it

- Sit on the edge of a sturdy chair with back straight and feet flat
- Place hands on hips or chair sides
- Activate core muscles
- Step right foot to the side, then left, alternating at a comfortable pace

2. Breathing

- Take a deep breath before beginning
- Exhale while stepping one foot to the side
- Inhale as you return the foot to its original position

3. Tips

- Maintain straight back
- Engage core for stability
- Focus on precise movements for cardiovascular health with safety

EASY

Seated Jumping Jacks

1 How to do it

- Sit in a stable chair with back straight, feet flat, engage core muscles

- Extend legs and lift arms into a 'V' shape

- Return to starting position in a steady rhythm

2 Breathing

- Breathe in while extending your legs and lifting your arms

- Breathe out as you come back to the center

3 Tips

- Emphasize controlled movements, focusing on arm and leg actions

- Position the chair against a wall or on a non-slip surface to ensure stability and safety

MEDIUM

Chair Sprints

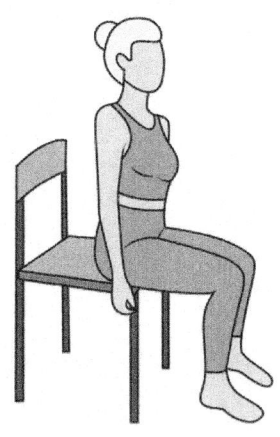

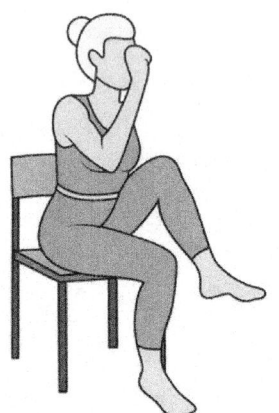

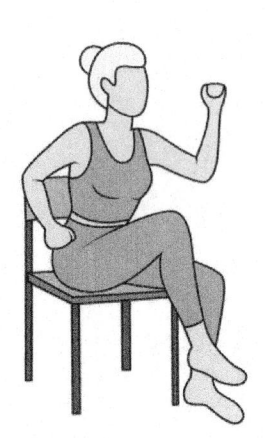

1. How to do it

- Position yourself at the front of a stable chair with your feet flat and hands resting on your thighs

- Activate your core, lean forward, and begin lifting your knees alternately as if running in one spot

- Sync your arm movements: swing the left arm forward as the right knee raises, and do the opposite for the other side

2. Breathing

- Establish a natural breathing rhythm

- Inhale during two knee lifts

- Exhale during the following two

3. Tips

- Maintain a straight spine without excessive rounding

- Focus on controlled movement rather than speed

- Improve chair stability by positioning it against a wall for increased safety

EASY

Arm Circles

1 How to do it

- Sit on a stable chair with feet flat, arms extended at shoulder level
- Rotate arms in circles, gradually increasing size, then switch direction
- For a challenge, speed up circles and add quick steps in place

2 Breathing

- Breathe in for four counts as you circle
- Breathe out for four counts, maintaining the movement.

3 Tips

- To maintain torso stability, engage your core muscles
- Ensure your shoulders are relaxed and avoid shrugging
- Focus on controlled and smooth movements

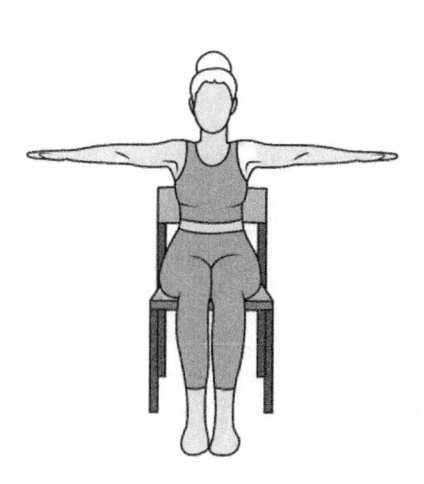

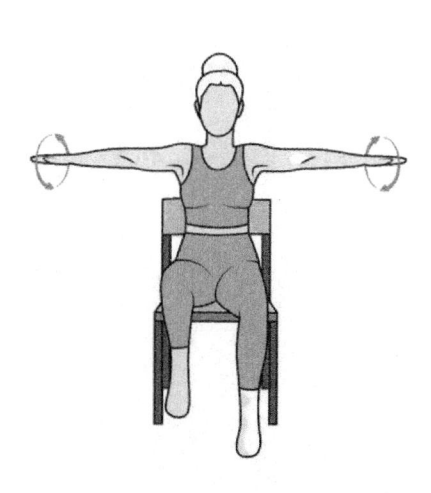

EASY

YOGA FOR SENIORS

Seated Side Leg Lifts

1. How to do it

- Sit up straight in a chair
- Engage core muscles, and take a deep breath
- Exhale as you lean forward
- Inhale as you return to an upright position, feeling the stretch

2. Breathing

- Begin by inhaling
- Exhale as you lean forward
- Inhale again to return to an upright position

3. Tips

- Keep your back straight, bending at the hips
- Engage your core muscles to maintain stability
- Perform the movement smoothly, avoiding sudden or hurried motions

MEDIUM

Seated Toe Touches

1. How to do it

- Sit upright in a chair with feet flat, engage core, and breathe deeply
- Lean forward as you exhale, stretching towards toes/shins/knees
- Inhale, engage core to return to upright position with hands up

2. Breathing

- Begin by inhaling
- Exhale as you lean forward
- Inhale as you return to an upright position

3. Tips

- Keep your back straight by hinging at your hips
- Engage your core for stability
- Perform the movement smoothly without any abrupt or hurried actions

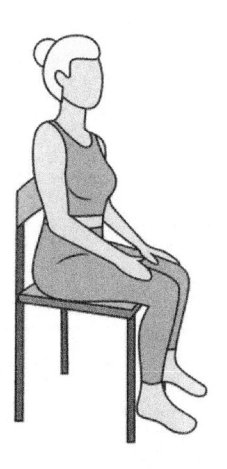

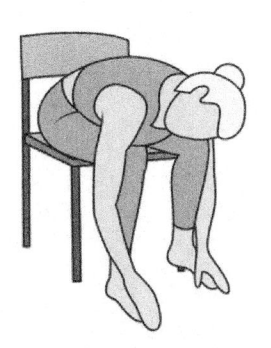

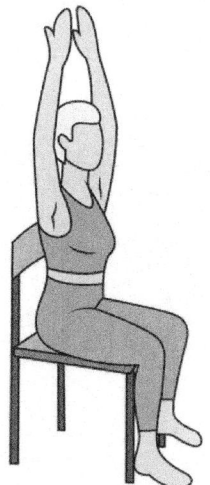

EASY

Chair Mountain Climbers

1. *How to do it*

- Stand an arm's length away from the chair, facing it. Place your hands on the seat of the chair, shoulder-width apart, creating a plank-like position angled downward

- Ensure your arms are straight and engage your core. Bring your right knee up towards your chest

- Lower your right foot back to the initial position. Raise your left knee towards your chest. Alternate between knees to simulate a climbing motion.

2. *Breathing*

- Breathe in as you raise the knee

- Breathe out as you lower the foot back down

3. *Tips*

- Maintain elongated spine

- Engage core for stability

- Use stable chair

EASY

MUSCLE TONING FOCUS

YOGA FOR SENIORS

Seated Overhead Press

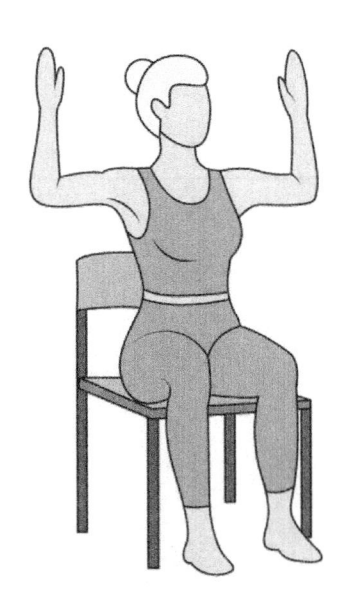

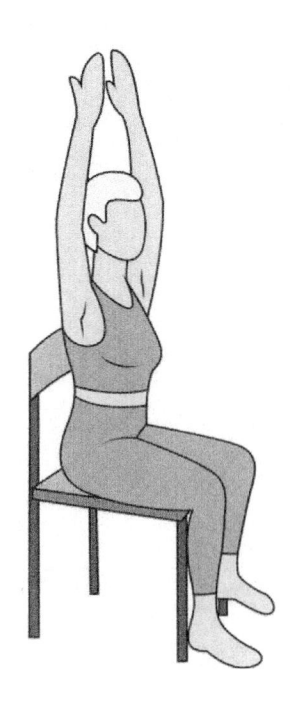

1 How to do it

- To start, sit upright in a sturdy chair with your feet flat on the floor and hip-width apart

- Create a "goalpost" shape by bending your elbows at shoulder height, with your palms facing forward

- Engage your core muscles, push your hands up overhead, and then return to the initial position

2 Breathing

- Take a deep breath before raising your hands above your head

- Exhale while pushing upward

- Inhale once more as you come back to the initial position

3 Tips

- Ensure your back is against the chair, avoiding any arching

- Relax your shoulders and focus on controlled movements. Adjust the range as necessary

EASY

YOGA FOR SENIORS

Chair Push-Ups

1. How to do it

- Position a stable chair against a wall and stand at arm's length
- Place hands shoulder-width apart on the chair seat, forming a diagonal line from head to heels
- Lower chest towards the chair, engage core, then push through palms to return.

2. Breathing

- Breathe in while bending your elbows to lower
- Breathe out as you push back up

3. Tips

- Keep elbows angled towards body
- Engage core for straight alignment
- Use higher surface for easier intensity

HARD

Seated Tummy Twists

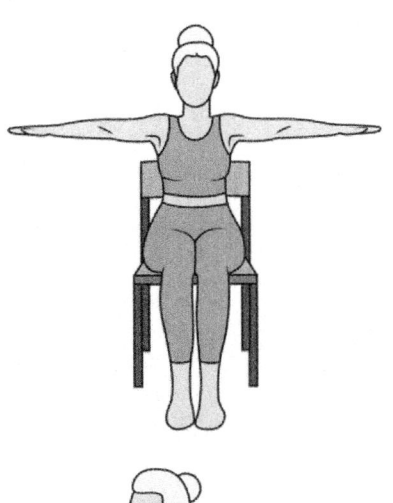

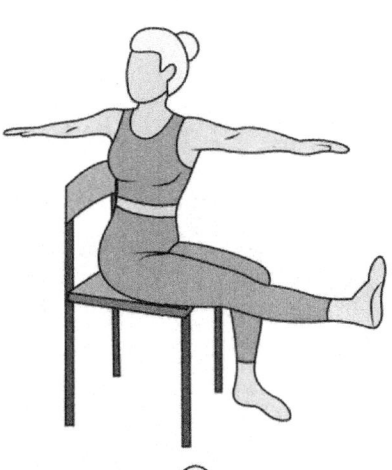

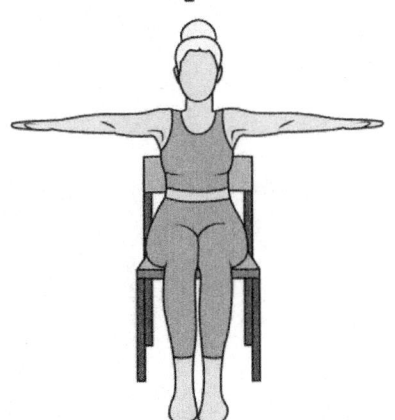

1. How to do it

- Sit upright on the front edge of a stable chair with feet flat and hip-width apart. Extend arms out to the sides at shoulder level with palms facing down while engaging your core

- Rotate your upper body to the right, raising your right leg parallel to the floor. Return to the center, then rotate to the left

- Perform this movement on each side to complete one repetition

2. Breathing

- Breathe in as you rotate right

- Breathe out as you retirn to the center

3. Tips

- To engage oblique muscles, rotate from the waist smoothly

- Avoid jerking, maintain controlled movements

- Twist comfortably without straining.

MEDIUM

Chair Squats

1. How to do it

- Stand in front of a chair, feet hip-width apart, arms extended for stability
- Activate core, bend knees, push hips back as if sitting down, then use leg muscles to stand up
- Use chair for support if needed

2. Breathing

- Breathe in as you lower your body
- Breathe out as you stand back up

3. Tips

- Keep a straight back and lifted chest
- Align knees with toes
- Sit gently on the chair, then progress to standing
- Secure chair against a wall or non-slip surface

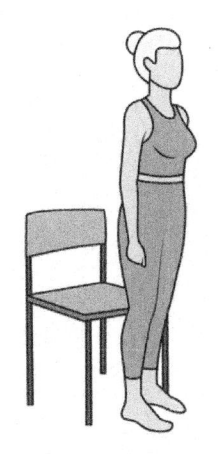

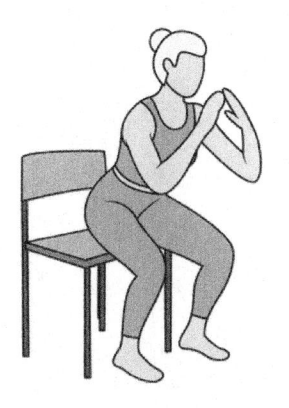

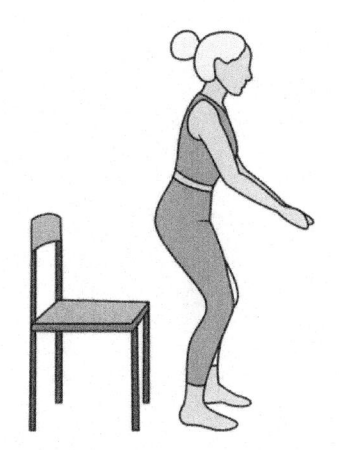

MEDIUM

YOGA FOR SENIORS

Seated Side Leg Lifts

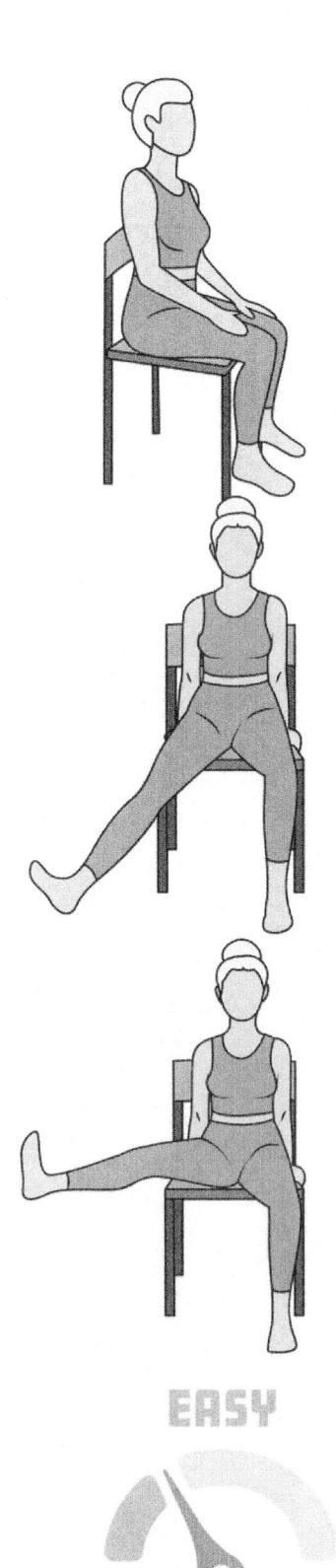

1. How to do it

- Sit firmly on a stable chair with your feet flat and hip-width apart, ensuring your back is straight and your core is engaged

- Extend your right leg slowly to the side, lifting it to a comfortable height

- Lower the leg without touching the floor and then lift it again. Repeat the same process with your left leg

2. Breathing

- Remember to inhale as you lift the leg

- Exhale as you lower it, ensuring it stays above the floor

3. Tips

- Keep an upright torso position without leaning

- Activate the outer thigh and hip muscles to maintain control

- Ensure the chair remains stable during the exercise

EASY

Seated Leg Curls

1 How to do it

- Sit on chair
- Extend legs
- Pull heels to buttocks
- Return to start

2 Breathing

- Breathe in while curling your heels
- Breathe out as you extend your legs

3 Tips

- Maintain good posture and move with control
- Keep your thighs stationary and only move your lower legs
- Adjust the intensity if you experience any knee problems or discomfort

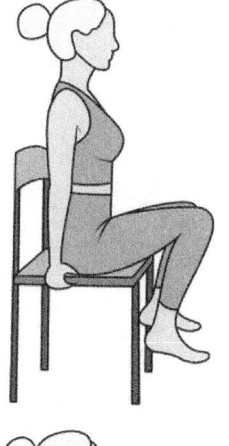

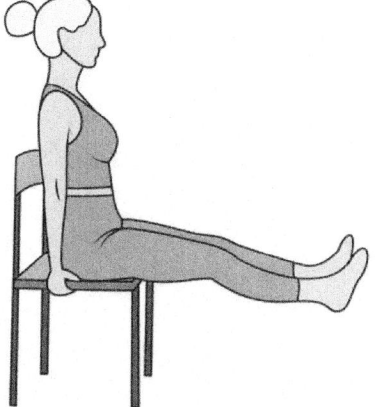

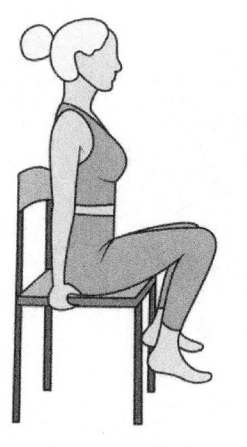

EASY

Seated Leg Presses

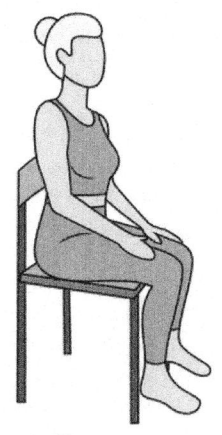

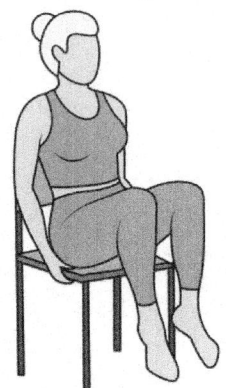

1. How to do it

- Position yourself upright in a stable chair, with your feet flat on the floor and hands resting on the chair's sides or in your lap

- Raise your feet slightly off the floor, bringing your knees towards your chest. Activate your core and thighs, then straighten your legs in front of you

- Bend your knees, bringing them back towards your chest to complete one repetition

2. Breathing

- Breathe in as you pull your knees toward your chest

- Breathe out as you straighten your legs

3. Tips

- Maintain contact with the chair's backrest

- Use core and thigh muscles to control movement

- Adjust foot height to engage thighs comfortably

HARD

Chair Dips

1. *How to do it*

- Sit on a stable chair
- Hold onto the sides
- Take steps forward, bend elbows to lower body to a 90-degree angle
- Then push back up while exhaling

2. *Breathing*

- Inhale when lowering your body
- Exhale when returning to the starting position

3. *Tips*

- Ensure chair stability on a non-slip surface
- Keep your back close to the chair to avoid strain
- Adjust foot placement for the desired challenge level
- Engage your core throughout for stability

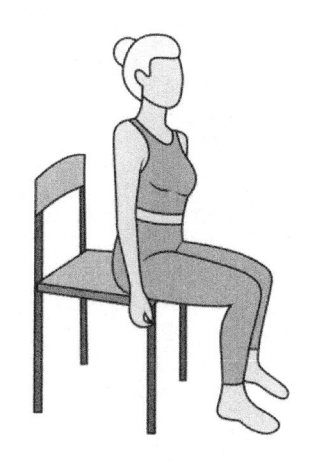

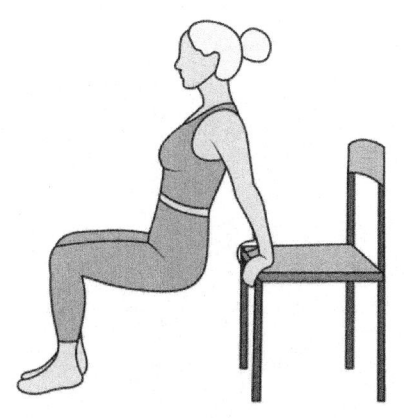

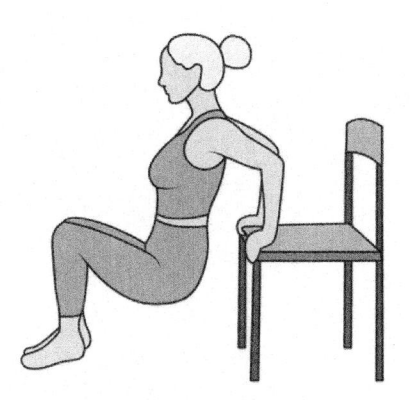

MEDIUM

Seated Cross Crunches

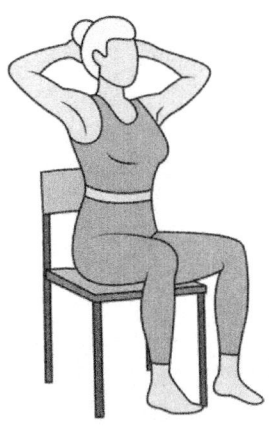

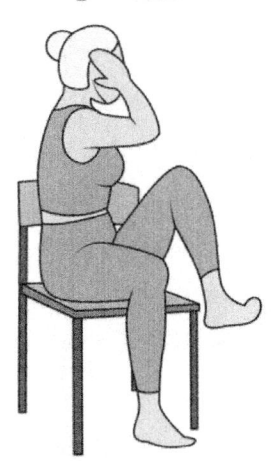

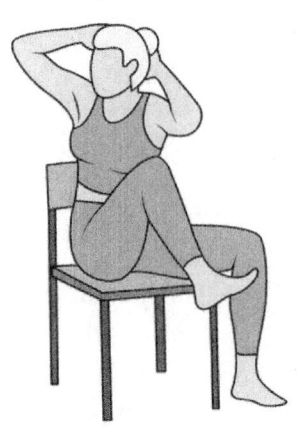

1. How to do it

- Begin by sitting upright in a chair with your feet flat on the floor, hip-width apart. Lightly place your fingertips behind your ears with elbows wide open

- Exhale as you raise your right knee and twist your torso, bringing your left elbow close to the knee

- Inhale as you return to the initial position, then switch sides and repeat the exercise

2. Breathing

- Breathe in at the starting position

- Breathe out while twisting

- Inhale as you come back to the center

3. Tips

- Keep your movements controlled and maintain a straight spine

- Refrain from straining your neck; let your fingertips assist but avoid pushing the movement

MEDIUM

Please
Give Us Your
FEEDBACK!

★★★★★

SCAN ME

A FREE BONUS IS WAITING YOU!

Join NOW our newsletter!

SCAN ME

CORE ACTIVATION AND BALANCE

YOGA FOR SENIORS

Seated Side Twists

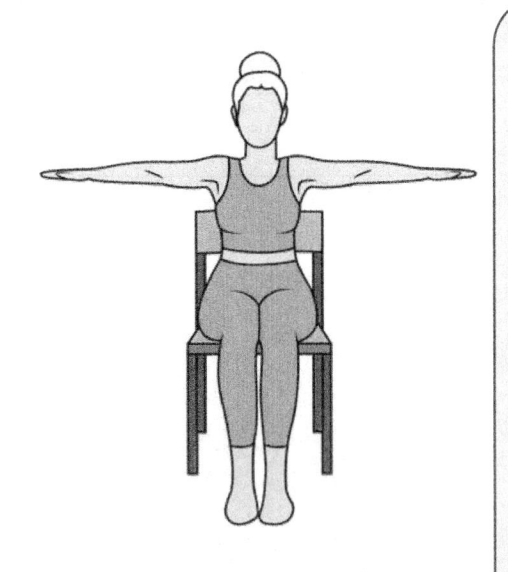

1. How to do it

- Sit upright in a stable chair with feet flat and hip-width apart, extending arms to the sides at shoulder level with palms facing down. Engage your core for good posture

- Slowly twist to the right with your right arm leading, and turn your head to look over your right shoulder to feel the stretch in your obliques and spine

- Return to the center and repeat the twist, this time to the left. Alternate between twisting to the right and left sides.

2. Breathing

- Take a deep breath at the center

- Exhale while twisting to the side

3. Tips

- Remember to move from your waist, not shoulders, keep hips forward, twist upper body

- Extend arms at shoulder level, prioritize control over speed for smooth movements.

MEDIUM

Standing Leg Curl

1. How to do it
- Stand behind a chair, feet hip-width apart
- Bend the right knee
- Hold briefly, then lower the foot
- Repeat on each leg.

2. Breathing
- Breathe in while getting ready to lift the foot
- Breathe out as you curl the leg upwards
- Inhale as you bring the leg back to the initial position.

3. Tips
- Maintain a straight spine at all times; refrain from leaning forward
- Activate the core muscles to enhance stability
- Concentrate on executing smooth, controlled movements to avoid any sudden jerks.

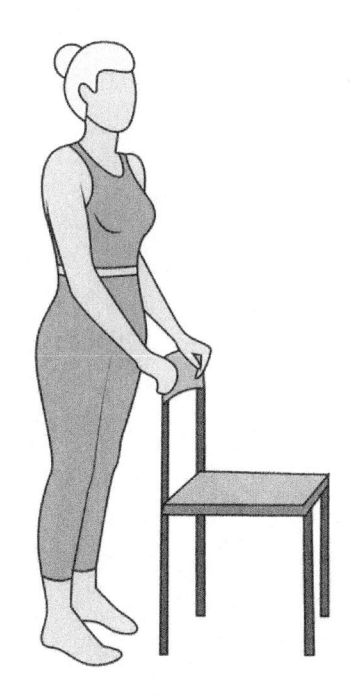

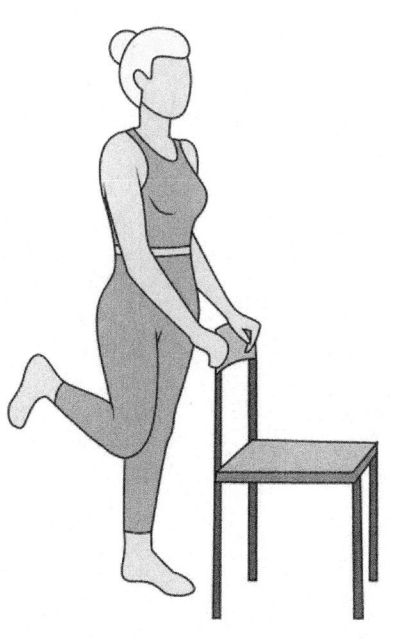

EASY

Seated Leg Extensions

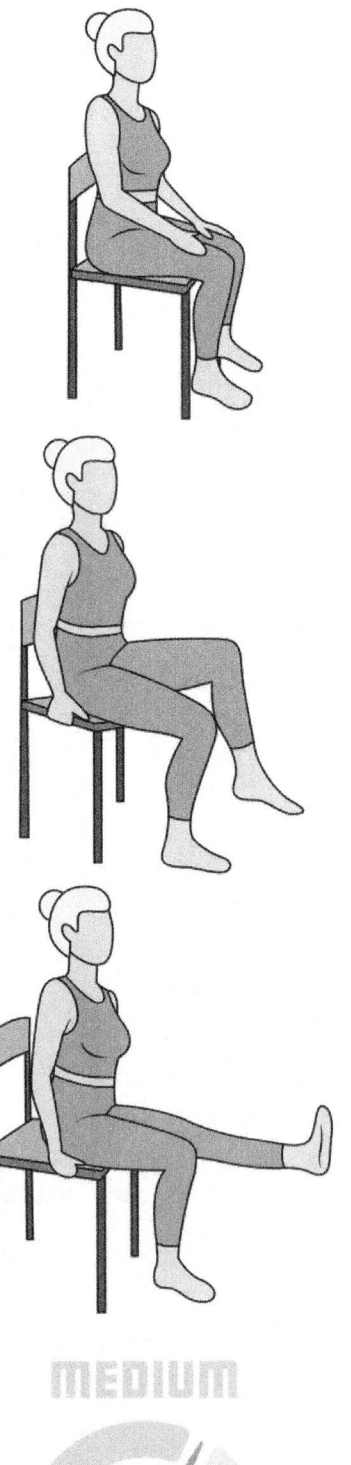

1 How to do it

- Sit upright in a stable chair with feet flat on the floor

- Keep hands on chair's sides or in lap, engage core muscles

- Lift right foot off the floor, straighten leg, hold

- Bend knee to lower foot, repeat with left leg

2 Breathing

- Remember to breathe in while extending your leg

- Breathe out when fully extended

- Inhale as you start to bend your knee

- Exhale as you return to the starting position.

3 Tips

- To maximize muscle engagement during leg extensions, maintain slow, controlled movements

- Keep the back straight, flex the foot with toes up, and use thigh muscles instead of momentum

MEDIUM

Chair Balance Lift

1 *How to do it*

- Sit upright in a sturdy chair with feet flat and hip-width apart

- Lift one foot off the floor, extend it forward, hold briefly for balance, then lower

- Repeat with the other leg

2 *Breathing*

- Breathe in as you raise your leg

- Breathe out as you lower it

3 *Tips*

- Ensure your back remains straight and avoid leaning

- Use your leg muscles and core to maintain balance

- Execute controlled movements and avoid sudden jerks

- Begin with shorter durations and slowly extend the hold time.

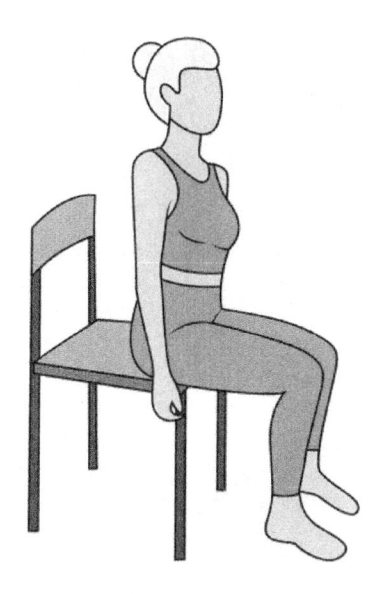

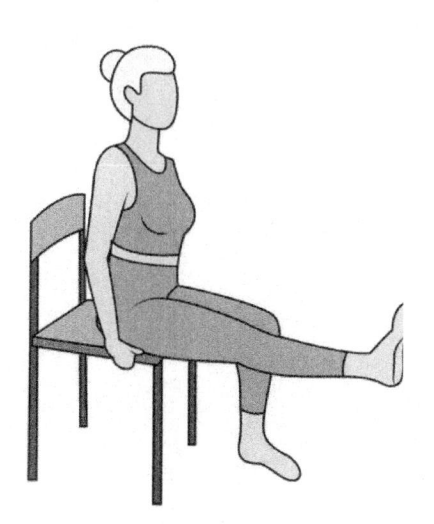

EASY

Seated Bicycle Crunches

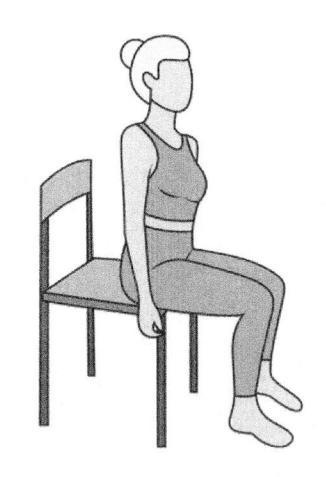

1. How to do it

- Sit firmly in a chair with feet flat, back straight
- Position fingertips behind ears, elbows out
- Lift right knee, twist torso to bring left elbow near knee
- Switch sides by lifting left knee and bringing right elbow towards it
- Alternate sides while repeating the exercise

2. Breathing

- Breathe in at the center
- Breathe out while twisting and bringing the opposite elbow towards the knee

3. Tips

- When rotating, engage your core, not just your shoulders
- Ensure your neck stays relaxed throughout the movement
- Maintain a slight lean to effectively activate your core muscles

HARD

Chair Boat Pose

1. How to do it

- Sit on chair edge with feet flat, hip-width apart
- Use chair sides for support, engage core, keep back straight
- Lean back slightly without rounding spine
- Lift both legs off floor, knees bent
- Chest open, shoulders relaxed, hold pose for a few breaths

2. Breathing

- Take a deep breath to get ready
- Exhale as you raise your legs and lean back
- Keep your breathing steady while holding the position

3. Tips

- Maintain steady movement to avoid jerking
- Keep back straight
- Widen chair grip for stability if needed

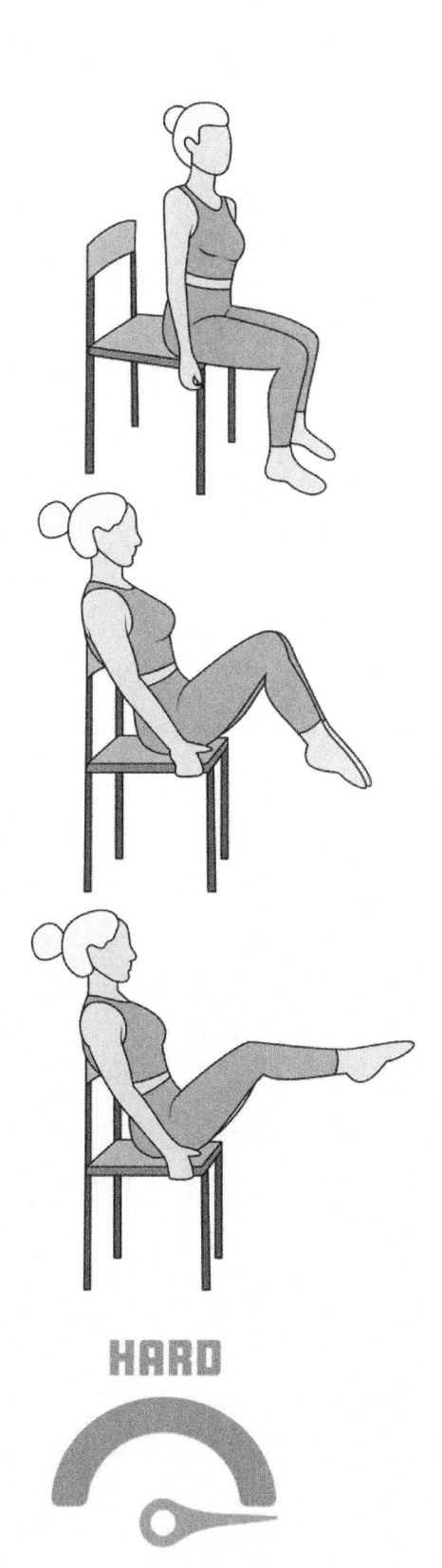

HARD

Seated Marches

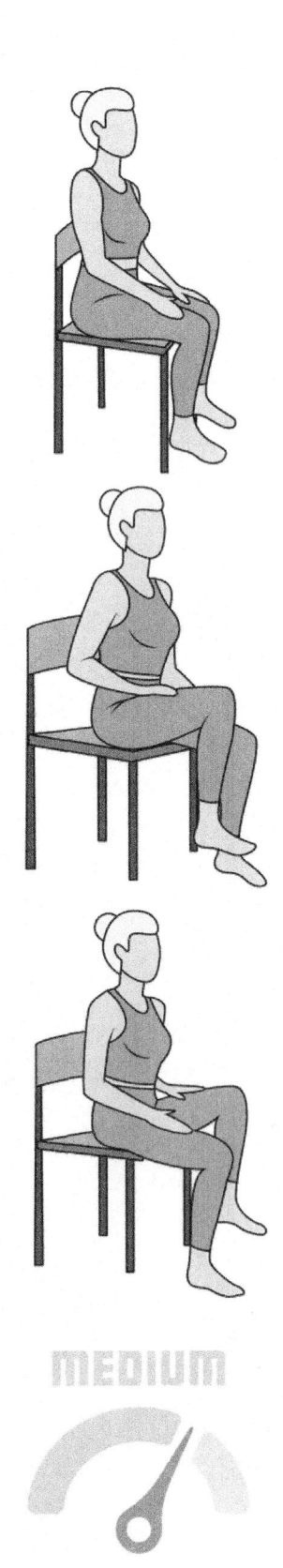

1. How to do it

- Sit upright in a chair
- Engage core muscles, and lift chest
- Alternate lifting knees towards chest in a marching motion while maintaining good posture

2. Breathing

- Remember to inhale while lifting your knee
- Exhale as you lower your foot

3. Tips

- Ensure smooth and controlled movements
- Keep your back straight and refrain from leaning back; rely on your core for stability
- Lift your knees to a comfortable height, activating your hip flexors and lower abs
- If you want to intensify the workout, increase your pace while staying in control

MEDIUM

Chair Taps

1. How to do it

- Sit upright on a stable chair with feet flat on the floor, hip-width apart

- Engage core muscles, lift toes of left foot towards ceiling, tap down, then repeat with right foot

- Alternate between left and right feet.

2. Breathing

- Take two taps while inhaling (one with each foot)

- Exhale during the next two taps

3. Tips

- Focus on engaging the muscles in the front of the shins (anterior tibialis)

- Maintain an upright posture without leaning back or slouching

- Lift your toes to a comfortable height without straining

- Keep your heels firmly planted on the ground

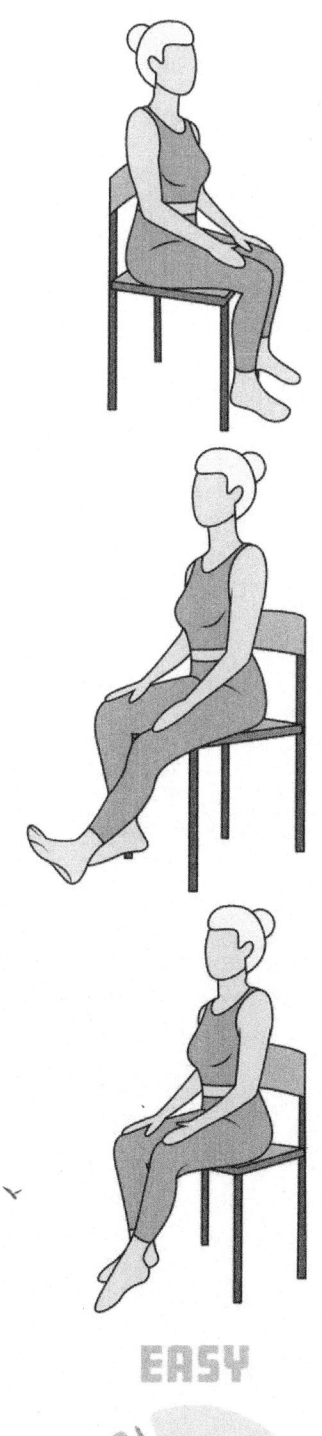

EASY

UPPER BODY STRENGTH AND FLEXIBILITY

Seated Star Twist

1. How to do it

- Sit in a chair with feet hip-width apart
- Twist body to the right, moving right foot to the side and extending arms overhead
- Pause in star twist pose, then return to starting position. Repeat on the left side

2. Breathing

- Inhale while stepping and raising arms
- pause in star twist, exhale back to initial position

3. Tips

- Ensure you maintain good posture and activate your core muscles
- Focus on executing smooth and controlled movements, avoiding sudden transitions

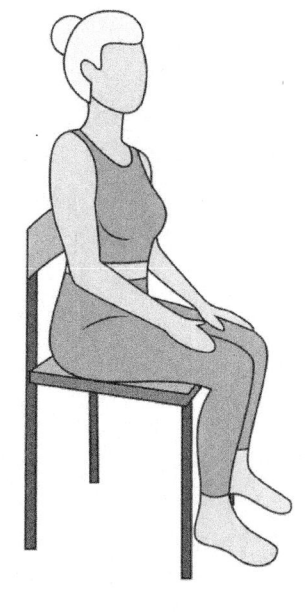

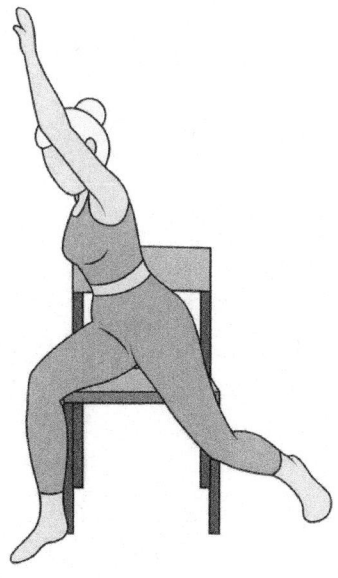

MEDIUM

YOGA FOR SENIORS

Seated Overhead Stretch

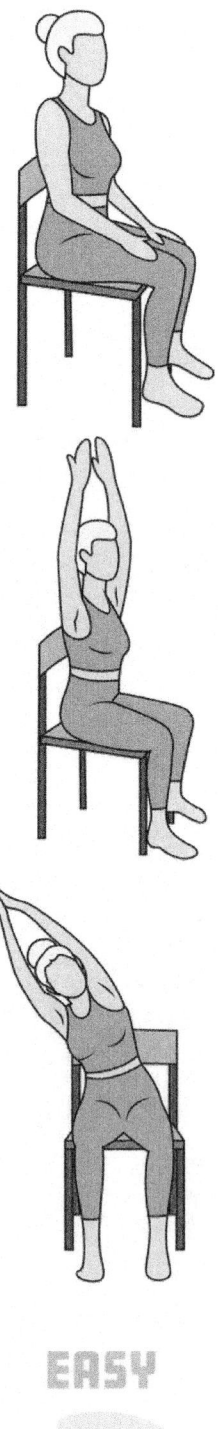

1. *How to do it*

- Sit in a chair with feet hip-width apart and hands at sides
- Move right foot to the side, twist upper body right, raise both arms
- Hold, return to start, lower arms
- Repeat on left side

2. *Breathing*

- Breathe in while stepping and lifting your arms
- Pause briefly, holding your breath in the star twist pose
- Exhale as you come back to the initial position

3. *Tips*

- Ensure you maintain good posture and activate your core muscles
- Focus on executing smooth and controlled movements, avoiding sudden or jerky transitions

EASY

Seated Bicep Stretch

1. *How to do it*

- Sit upright in your chair and extend your arms out to the sides with palms facing forward

- Rotate your arms so that your thumbs point backward and palms face away from you

- Slowly pull your arms back to feel a stretch in your biceps

2. *Breathing*

- Extend your arms to the side while inhaling

- Rotate and stretch your arms back while exhaling

3. *Tips*

- Maintain an upright spine and refrain from leaning forward

- Make sure the movement is gentle to prevent over-stretching

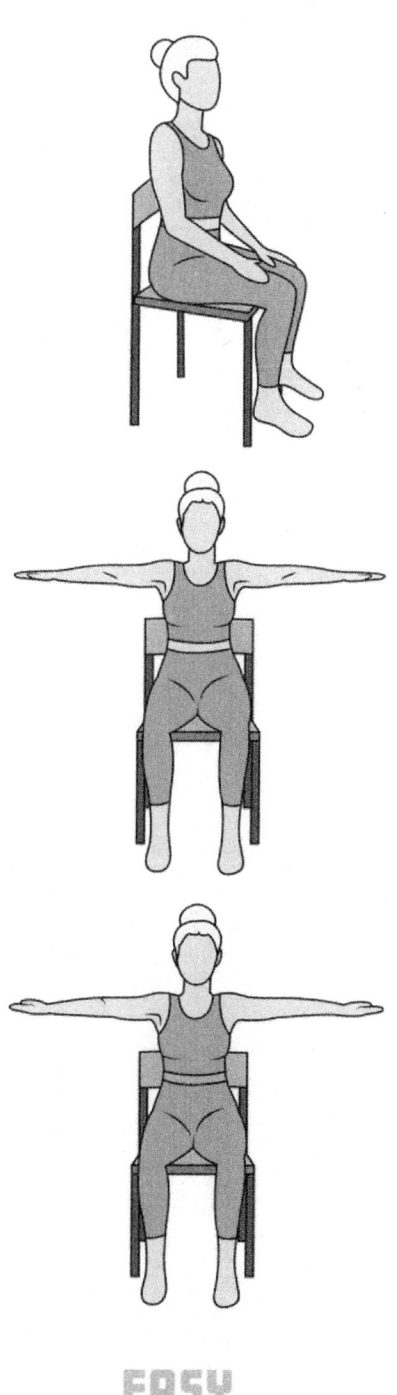

EASY

YOGA FOR SENIORS

Chair Tricep Stretch

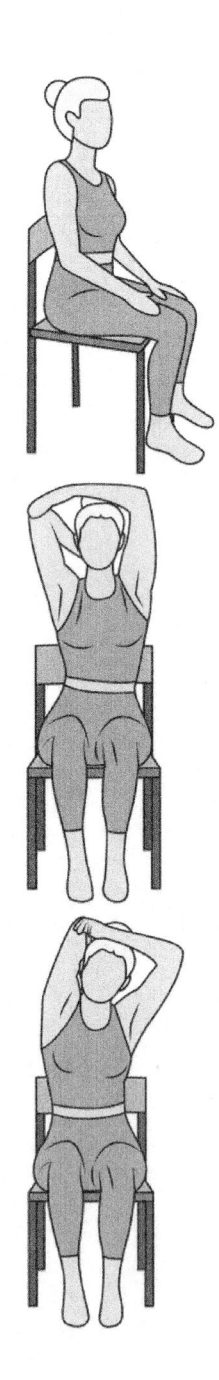

1. How to do it

- Maintain upright posture with feet flat
- Raise right arm above head and bend elbow toward upper back
- Use left hand to gently push on right elbow for a deeper stretch
- Hold for a few breaths before switching sides.

2. Breathing

- Breathe in as you lift your arm above your head
- Breathe out while bending your elbow to deepen the stretch

3. Tips

- Keep your head upright and avoid leaning forward
- Use a gentle touch and refrain from applying excessive pressure on the elbow

EASY

Seated Chest Expansion

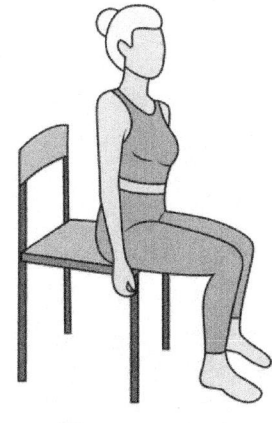

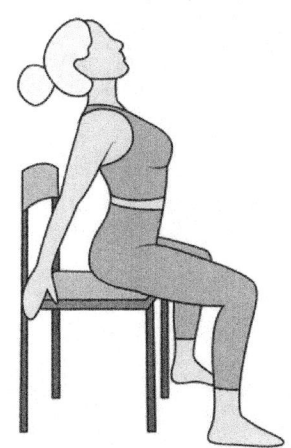

1. How to do it

- Sit at the front of your chair with feet flat
- Interlock fingers behind back with palms facing
- Raise arms to expand chest, take deep breaths, then relax.

2. Breathing

- Take a deep breath while opening your chest
- Exhale while holding the position
- Inhale as you release the stretch

3. Tips

- To prevent overarching the lower back,
- Remember to keep the chin slightly tucked to avoid straining the neck

EASY

Please
Give Us Your
FEEDBACK!

★★★★★

SCAN ME

A FREE BONUS IS WAITING YOU!

Join NOW our newsletter!

SCAN ME

LOWER BODY STRENGTH AND FLEXIBILITY

Seated Leg Lifts

1 *How to do it*

- Sit upright on a sturdy chair
- Hold the chair for stability
- Extend left leg parallel to the floor, hold for 3 seconds
- Lower without touching the floor, then raise
- Repeat 10 times per leg

2 *Breathing*

- Take a deep breath when your leg is on the floor
- Gradually exhale lifting your leg
- Inhale as you lower your leg without touching the floor

3 *Tips*

- Maintain upright posture, engage core for stability
- Adjust leg height for comfort if needed

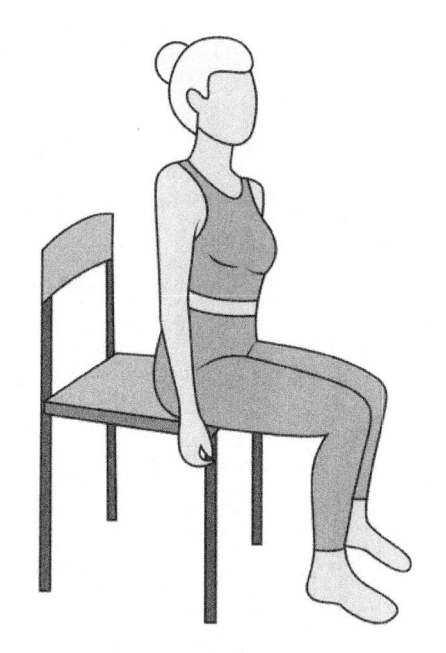

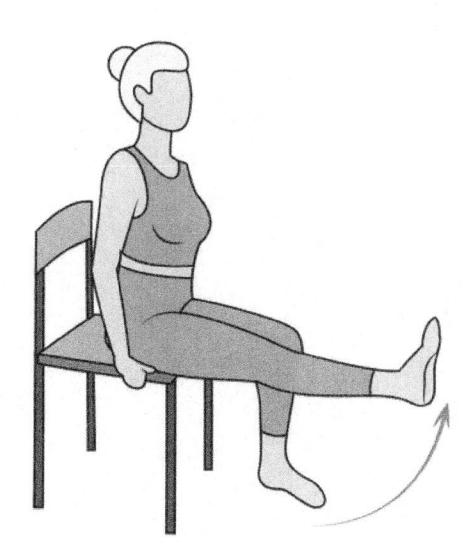

EASY

Hamstring Stretch

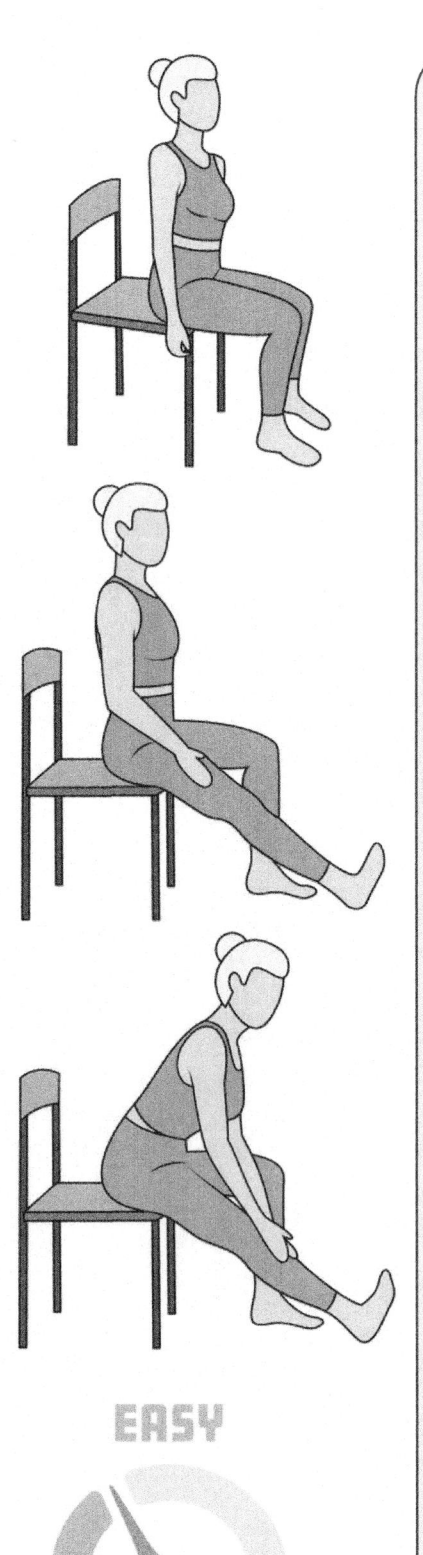

1. How to do it

- Sit at the edge of a stable chair with your back upright
- Extend right leg forward, keeping heel on ground and toes up
- Lean forward from hips with straight back, stretching arms towards leg
- Hold for 30 seconds, then switch legs

2. Breathing

- Inhale deeply
- Lean forward while exhaling to stretch, hold while inhaling
- Return to initial position while exhaling

3. Tips

- Maintain a straight back while bending at the hips
- Strive for a gentle stretch without overexerting; avoid any pain
- Concentrate on stretching your hamstrings

EASY

Chair Pigeon Pose

1. How to do it

- Sit in a stable chair with feet flat on the floor
- Cross right ankle over left thigh, lean forward at hips to stretch right hip and glutes for 30 seconds
- Switch legs

2. Breathing

- Breathe in deeply as you prepare for the stretch
- Exhale while leaning forward
- Keep your breathing steady
- Exhale as you return to the starting position

3. Tips

- Flex your foot on the bent leg to protect the knee
- Ease into the stretch
- Keep an upright spine

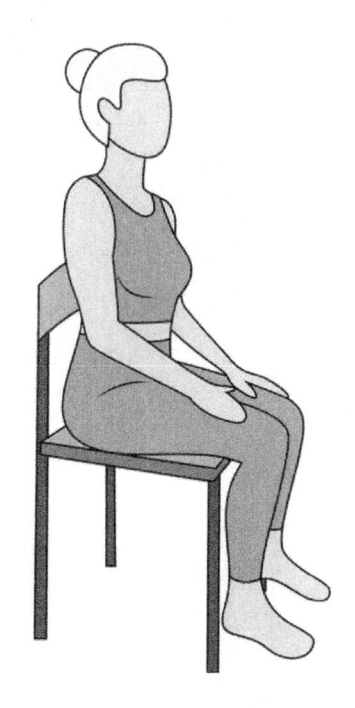

MEDIUM

YOGA FOR SENIORS

Chair Ankle Flex

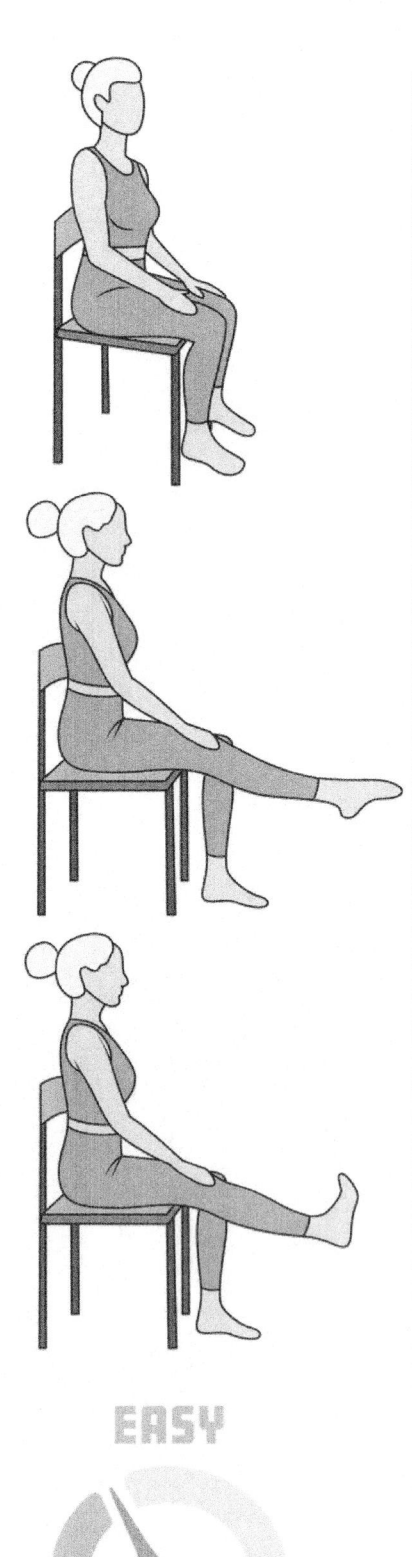

1. How to do it

- Begin by sitting upright in a chair, ensuring your feet are flat on the floor and your hands are resting on your thighs

- Raise your right leg a few inches off the floor. Point your toes outward, then flex them back towards your shin

- Perform this pointing and flexing action 10 times. Lower your right leg and switch to the left

2. Breathing

- Inhale deeply, flex foot pulling toes towards shin

- Exhale slowly, extend toes away to stretch the top of the foot

3. Tips

- Keep the lifted leg's knee straight but not locked

- Engage thigh muscles for knee support

- Focus on precise movements for full ankle range of motion.

EASY

Seated Calf Raises

1. How to do it

- Sit up straight in a chair, engage core muscles
- Lift heels off the ground targeting calf muscles
- Lower them slowly
- Repeat for desired repetitions.

2. Breathing

- Breathe in as you get ready to raise your heels
- Breathe out while lifting your heels
- Inhale as you lower your heels back down

3. Tips

- To maintain controlled motion, avoid jerking
- Elevate heels high for calf muscles
- Engage thighs and core for stability during the exercise

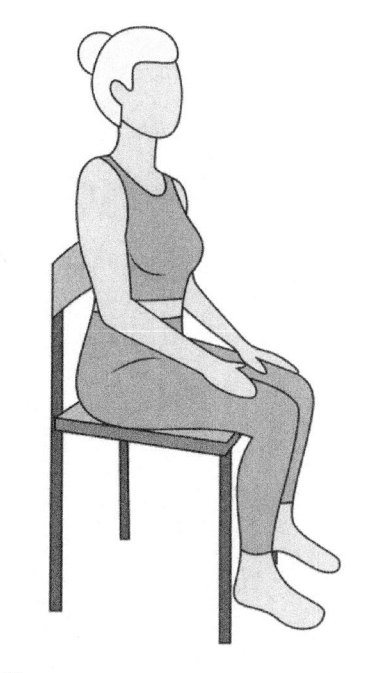

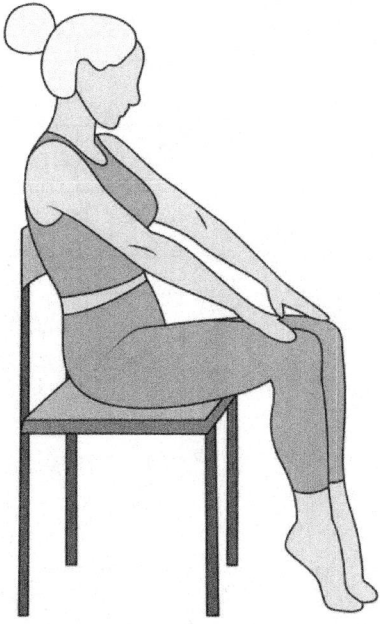

EASY

28-Days Plan: Full Body Mobility

- **Beginners:** 10 repetitions for 2 sets
- **Intermediate:** 15 repetitions for 3 sets
- **Advanced:** 20 repetitions for 4 sets

DAY 1-8-15-22
SEQUENCES
Neck Extension and Flexion
Seated Neck Turn
Seated Leg Lifts
Seated Overhead Press
Standing Leg Curl
Seated Chest Expansion
Twist and Shout

DAY 2-9-16-23
SEQUENCES
Seated Neck Tilt
Seated Shoulder Roll
Hamstring Stretch
Seated Side Leg Lifts
Chair Balance Lift
Seated Overhead Stretch
Seated Side Steps

DAY 3-10-17-24
SEQUENCES
Cross-Body Arm Stretch
Chair Eagle Arms
Chair Ankle Flex
Seated Leg Curls
Chair Taps
Seated Bicep Stretch
Chair Sprints

DAY 4-11-18-25
SEQUENCES
Cross-Body Arm Stretch
Seated Ankle Rotations
Chair Ankle Flex
Seated Side Leg Lifts
Standing Leg Curl
Chair Tricep Stretch
Twist and Shout

28-Days Plan: Full Body Mobility

- **Beginners:** 10 repetitions for 2 sets
- **Intermediate:** 15 repetitions for 3 sets
- **Advanced:** 20 repetitions for 4 sets

DAY 5-12-19-26
SEQUENCES
Seated Neck Turn
Side-Seated Chair Twist
Seated Leg Lifts
Seated Leg Curls
Chair Taps
Seated Overhead Stretch
Arm Circles

DAY 6-13-20-27
SEQUENCES
Seated Shoulder Roll
Sit-Ankle Stretch
Hamstring Stretch
Seated Overhead Press
Chair Balance Lift
Seated Bicep Stretch
Chair Sprints

DAY 7-14-21-28
SEQUENCES
Chair Eagle Arms
Side-Seated Chair Twist
Seated Calf Raises
Seated Overhead Press
Chair Balance Lift
Seated Overhead Stretch
Chair Sprints

28-Days Plan: Weight Loss

- **Beginners:** 10 repetitions for 2 sets
- **Intermediate:** 15 repetitions for 3 sets
- **Advanced:** 20 repetitions for 4 sets

DAY 1-8-15-22
WARM-UP SEQUENCES
Seated Ankle Rotations
Seated Chair Twist
Sit-Ankle Stretch
CARDIO BOOSTERS
Seated Side Steps
Chair Sprints
Arm Circles
Seated Toe Touches

DAY 2-9-16-23
WARM-UP SEQUENCES
Cross-Body Arm Stretch
Chair Eagle Arms
Side-Seated Chair Twist
CARDIO BOOSTERS
Chair Mountain Climbers
Seated Leg Swings
Twist and Shout
Seated Side Steps

DAY 3-10-17-24
WARM-UP SEQUENCES
Seated Neck Turn
Seated Neck Tilt
Seated Shoulder Roll
CARDIO BOOSTERS
Chair Mountain Climbers
Twist and Shout
Chair Sprints
Seated Toe Touches

DAY 4-11-18-25
WARM-UP SEQUENCES
Neck Extension and Flexion
Seated Neck Tilt
Chair Eagle Arms
CARDIO BOOSTERS
Chair Mountain Climbers
Seated Leg Swings
Seated Side Steps
Arm Circles

28-Days Plan: Weight Loss

- **Beginners:** 10 repetitions for 2 sets
- **Intermediate:** 15 repetitions for 3 sets
- **Advanced:** 20 repetitions for 4 sets

DAY 5-12-19-26
WARM-UP SEQUENCES
Seated Neck Tilt
Cross-Body Arm Stretch
Seated Ankle Rotations
CARDIO BOOSTERS
Twist and Shout
Seated Side Steps
Chair Sprints
Seated Toe Touches

DAY 6-13-20-27
WARM-UP SEQUENCES
Seated Neck Turn
Chair Eagle Arms
Sit-Ankle Stretch
CARDIO BOOSTERS
Chair Mountain Climbers
Seated Leg Swings
Seated Side Steps
Arm Circles

DAY 7-14-21-28
WARM-UP SEQUENCES
Seated Shoulder Roll
Cross-Body Arm Stretch
Chair Eagle Arms
CARDIO BOOSTERS
Seated Leg Swings
Twist and Shout
Seated Side Steps
Seated Toe Touches

28-Days Plan: Weight Loss

- **Beginners:** 10 repetitions for 2 sets
- **Intermediate:** 15 repetitions for 3 sets
- **Advanced:** 20 repetitions for 4 sets

DAY 5-12-19-26
WARM-UP SEQUENCES
Seated Neck Tilt
Cross-Body Arm Stretch
Seated Ankle Rotations
CARDIO BOOSTERS
Twist and Shout
Seated Side Steps
Chair Sprints
Seated Toe Touches

DAY 6-13-20-27
WARM-UP SEQUENCES
Seated Neck Turn
Chair Eagle Arms
Sit-Ankle Stretch
CARDIO BOOSTERS
Chair Mountain Climbers
Seated Leg Swings
Seated Side Steps
Arm Circles

DAY 7-14-21-28
WARM-UP SEQUENCES
Seated Shoulder Roll
Cross-Body Arm Stretch
Chair Eagle Arms
CARDIO BOOSTERS
Seated Leg Swings
Twist and Shout
Seated Side Steps
Seated Toe Touches

Please Give Us Your **FEEDBACK!**

★ ★ ★ ★ ★

SCAN ME

A FREE BONUS IS WAITING YOU!

Join **NOW** our newsletter!

SCAN ME

Printed in Great Britain
by Amazon